America's Game
Minnesota Twins

Paul Joseph

ABDO & Daughters
PUBLISHING

Published by Abdo & Daughters, 4940 Viking Dr., Suite 622, Edina, MN 55435.

Copyright ©1997 by Abdo Consulting Group, Inc., Pentagon Tower, P.O. Box 36036, Minneapolis, Minnesota 55435. International copyrights reserved in all countries. No part of this book may be reproduced in any form without written permission from the publisher. Printed in the United States.

Cover photo: Allsport
Interior photos: Wide World Photo, pages 1, 5, 9, 10, 14-17, 21-23, 25, 27.

Edited by Kal Gronvall

Library of Congress Cataloging-in-Publication Data

Joseph, Paul, 1970-
    Minnesota Twins / Paul Joseph
        p. cm. — (America's game)
    Includes index.
    Summary: Focuses on key players and events in the history of the Minnesota Twins, formerly know as the Washington Senators.
    ISBN 1-56239-670-6
    1. Minnesota Twins (Baseball team)—History—Juvenile literature. [1. Minnesota Twins (Baseball team) 2. Baseball—History.]
    I. Title. II. Series.
    GV875.M55J67   1997
    796.357'64'09776579—dc20   96-22380
                                                                            CIP
                                                                            AC

Contents

Minnesota Twins

Most people don't know that the Minnesota Twins' original franchise has been in operation since 1901. They were the founding members of baseball's American League. Today's Twins started out in Washington, D.C., as the Senators, and went by that name until they moved to Minnesota in 1961.

The Minnesota Twins franchise has had more than its share of low points in its lengthy history. But the high points are so thrilling that baseball fans forget the bad and remember the good.

The Twins captured two record-filled, seven-game World Series wins in less than five years (1987 and 1991). And who could forget their greatest record in franchise history? In 1965, Minnesota won 102 games, marking the first time the Twins reached the World Series.

Before 1961, the Washington Senators were World Series Champions in 1924. They returned to the World Series the next year, only to lose. The Senators' third and last World Series appearance was in 1933, but they lost in five games.

Facing page: Kirby Puckett hits a solo home run in Game 3 of the 1991 World Series against the Atlanta Braves.

Baseball fans will always remember the players who made those great moments possible, like sluggers Leon Goslin, Harmon Killebrew, and Kent Hrbek. Great pitchers like Walter "Big Train" Johnson, Jim Kaat, Frank Viola, and Jack Morris also are part of the team's legacy. And then came the clutch hitting of Tony Oliva and Rod Carew, who combined for 10 batting titles. But the player who did it all, and will be remembered as the greatest Twins player ever, is Kirby Puckett.

These great players are the main reason Twins fans remember the good and forget the bad.

The Washington Senators

On December 7, 1900, the Washington Senators franchise was born. The team played in the newly-formed, eight-team American League (AL). The AL then was considered second class to the powerful National League (NL).

Early on, the Senators were a dismal team. Washington, D.C., became known as "first in war, first in peace, and last in the American League." They were not only last in wins, but last in most team categories.

One bright spot in the Senators' camp came in 1902. That's when NL star Ed Delahanty signed with the Senators. In his first year, he batted .376 and won the AL batting crown.

Even though he signed a three-year contract , Delahanty wanted more money from the Senators. Neither Delahanty nor the Senators' management would budge, and Delahanty left the team during a road trip and headed home. Two days later, Delahanty's dead body was found several miles below a bridge. Nobody knows if he fell, jumped, or was pushed from the bridge. Delahanty's death remains one of the biggest mysteries in baseball history.

Walter "Big Train" Johnson

After losing their star hitter, Washington finished last in every category. Then, in 1907, the Senators signed the greatest pitcher in franchise history. In fact, Walter "Big Train" Johnson became one of the best pitchers to ever play Major League Baseball.

He was called the "Big Train" because his fastball came in so hard and fast, it was like a speeding locomotive. Whenever Johnson pitched, the other team was in trouble. Johnson's earned run average (ERA) was excellent.

Even though Johnson was a powerful pitcher, the Senators couldn't win many games. The problem? The team couldn't score runs. Because of the poor offense, Johnson lost many games 1-0 or 2-1.

Johnson's career, which extended from 1907 to 1927, was still outstanding. Big Train had 416 AL wins, a record that still stands today. He is second in wins to Cy Young, who played in both the American and National Leagues. Many people believe that Johnson would have surpassed Young had he played on a better team.

Big Train has the most career shutouts with 110. He still ranks in the top 10 with a 2.17 ERA, 3,509 strikeouts, and 531 complete games.

Johnson threw 55 consecutive innings without giving up a run, a record that stood until 1968. To this day, only two other pitchers have surpassed that mark.

Walter "Big Train" Johnson warming up before a game.

Championship Seasons

In the Senators' first 23 years, losing was a tradition. A few times, they actually captured a second-place finish. Finally, in 1924, the team put it all together.

Leon "Goose" Goslin threw right-handed and hit left-handed.

Big Train led the team in pitching with 6 shutouts, 23 wins, and 158 strikeouts. This time, Johnson was supported by the league's best pitching staff. With the hitting of Leon "Goose" Goslin, Bucky Harris, and Joe Judge—all of whom batted over .300—the team captured the AL title. For the first time, the Senators were headed to the World Series.

The Senators-Giants 1924 World Series was a Series to remember. To the surprise and shock of many, Johnson lost his first two Series starts. But that didn't stop the Senators. They pushed the Series to a seventh and deciding game, giving Big Train one last chance to capture a victory and make the Senators World Champions.

The Senators rallied in the 8th inning to tie the game 3-3. The two teams remained deadlocked until the 12th inning. Johnson retired the side with his fastball. Then, in the bottom of the 12th inning, the Senators punched in the winning run. They were finally World Champions. Walter Johnson had won the biggest game of his career.

The determined Senators made it back to the World Series the following year. This time, Johnson won his first two starts, and the Senators had a 3-1 Series lead over the Pittsburgh Pirates.

The Pirates fought back and tied the Series, sending it into another seventh game. Big Train again got the start. This time, the ending wasn't so sweet. The Senators lost a heartbreaker 9-7.

After that season, the Senators faded. Walter Johnson retired after the 1927 season, ending one of the greatest careers in baseball history.

Johnson managed the Senators from 1929 to 1932, but had little success. In 1936, he was among the first five players elected to the Baseball Hall of Fame.

Back To The Bottom

In 1933, the Senators returned to the limelight. With some excellent trades for good pitching, the Senators won the American League and headed to their third World Series in 10 years.

They ran into National League Champion New York Giants. The Senators were no match for the overpowering Giants, losing in a lopsided five-game Series.

That 10-year span was the highlight for the Washington Senators. It wasn't until 1942 that they again seriously contended for the AL crown, finishing in second place. But by 1944, they had returned to the cellar again.

The 1950s were the lowest of lows for the franchise. Not only did they play poorly, they had the lowest attendance in the major leagues.

Owner Calvin Griffith, whose family had been associated with the Senators since their first season, knew something had to be done or the franchise wouldn't be around in the 1960s.

Griffith made trades, picked up players, and developed some of the best young talent in the league. But the biggest move came in October 1960, when the Senators got a new name and a new place to play.

A Stunning Move

After receiving approval from the American League, Griffith completed one of the most stunning franchise moves in baseball history. The "Twin Cities" of Minneapolis and St. Paul, Minnesota, were ready for a major league franchise. They became the new home of the Senators. Along with a new home came a new name.

The Minnesota Twins were named after the Twin Cities that claimed them. The team began its first season on April 11, 1961. Playing in New York against the defending AL Champion Yankees, the Twins crushed the champs 6-0.

Although the Twins finished in 7th place, they drew some 1.3 million fans to the ballpark. The fans didn't get to see many wins, but they did get to see some exciting players with great promise.

One of these young stars was Harmon Killebrew, who finished the season with 31 home runs. The Twins also had Bob Allison, who won the AL Rookie of the Year Award two years earlier. Behind the plate was hard-hitting catcher Jim Lemon. At second base was Billy Martin. The Twins also had the awesome pitching duo of Jim Kaat and Camilo Pascual.

Minnesota baseball fans were very loyal, and continued to support their Twins. They were patient, too. They knew it was only a matter of time before their team would be on top of the American League.

Minnesota Twins'
slugging great
Harmon Killebrew.

Making The Climb

The Twins began to come alive in 1962. Led by clutch hitting and powerful pitching, Minnesota started to make their climb. They finished in second place that year, battling the Yankees all the way. In 1962, the Twins finished first in total attendance, giving Griffith a real reason to smile.

The fans got their money's worth that season with wins and great players. Killebrew was tops in the league in homers with 48 and RBIs with 126, outshining the two star sluggers of that era, Roger Maris and Mickey Mantle.

Camilo Pascual and Jim Kaat had outstanding pitching performances, combining for 38 wins. Pascual led the league in strikeouts, shutouts, and complete games. Kaat finished the year with the team-low ERA.

In 1963, the Twins had another solid year. Teams around the league feared their powerful hitting. Killebrew again led the league in homers with 45. With other sluggers Bob Allison, Jimmie Hall, and Earl Batty, the Twins hit the highest number of homers in baseball that year—225. Although they finished third, they still won an impressive 91 games.

In 1964, the Twins started rookie Tony Oliva. Tony became one of the greatest hitters in baseball history. In his first season, he led the league in runs (109), hits (217), and batting average (.323). He also pounded 32 home runs. For his efforts, Oliva was named Rookie of the Year.

The Twins again led the league in team home runs with 221. For the third straight year, Killebrew was the league's home run champion with 49.

Minnesota finally made it to the top in 1965. They had their best regular season in franchise history, winning more than 100 games!

Twins' outfielder Tony Oliva.

The 1965 World Series

In 1965, Oliva was the league batting champ for the second straight year. Gold Glove shortstop Zoilo Versalles scored 126 runs and was named the league's Most Valuable Player (MVP). Meanwhile, the baseballs kept flying out of the park. Killebrew, Hall, Allison, and Don Mincher each had 20-plus home runs.

The Minnesota Twins ran away with the American League crown, finishing the 1965 season with a 102-60 record, and 7 games ahead of the second-place team. Now they would face the mighty Los Angeles Dodgers. They had one of the best pitching duos in all of baseball: Sandy Koufax and Don Drysdale.

The Twins had some talented pitchers of their own. Kaat and Pascual were performing well. Jim "Mudcat" Grant, acquired from the Cleveland Indians, led the team with a 21-7 record.

Baseball fans expected an exciting World Series. They were not disappointed. In the first two games in Minnesota, the Twins hit well and pitched even better, winning 8-2 and 5-1.

Outfielder Bob Allison makes a diving catch against the Los Angeles Dodgers in Game 2 of the 1965 World Series.

Twins' pitcher Jim Grant hits a game-winning three-run homer in Game 6 of the 1965 World Series.

The Series moved to the West Coast, where the Dodgers picked up three wins behind the outstanding pitching of Koufax and Drysdale.

Back in Minnesota, the Twins tied the series 3-3 behind Grant's amazing performance. Not only did he toss a six-hitter, he hit a game-winning, three-run homer. That sent the Series to a seventh and deciding game.

Koufax was on the hill for the Dodgers, and Kaat for the Twins. The two teams didn't need their bats because Koufax and Kaat began a pitching duel. Unfortunately for the Twins, Koufax pitched his second shutout, striking out 10 batters. He had an incredible 0.38 Series ERA and picked up the World Series MVP. The Twins' talented hitters could only muster a .195 batting average against the overpowering Koufax. Despite the World Series loss, the 1965 season remains one of the greatest in Minnesota Twins history.

Pitcher Walter "Big Train" Johnson had a record 416 AL wins before retiring in 1927.

In 1924, Leon "Goose" Goslin helped the Washington Senators capture the AL title.

In 1964, slugger Harmon Killebrew was the AL home run champion with 49.

Tony Oliva, 1964 Rookie of the Year.

Rod Carew, winner of the 1967 Rookie of the Year Award, and the 1977 AL MVP.

First baseman Kent Hrbek, hero of Game 6 of the 1987 World Series.

1987 World Series MVP Frank "Sweet Music" Viola.

Kirby Puckett led the Twins to World Championship seasons in 1987 and 1991.

Great Talent, No World Series

In 1967, the Twins added another future Hall-of-Famer to their lineup. Rod Carew went on to win the Rookie of the Year Award that season. He would finish his career as the greatest hitter in Twins history, winning seven batting titles, and the league's MVP Award in 1977.

As a rookie, Carew tried to lead his team to another World Series. With a nice cushion in the American League standings, the Twins slumped in September and finished one game behind the Boston Red Sox.

Divisional play began in 1969, and the Twins were now in the AL West. Minnesota won the first-ever AL West title that year with some great offensive talent. American League MVP Harmon Killebrew led the league in homers and RBIs. Rod Carew won the batting title. Rich Reese and Tony Oliva each batted over .300.

In the series for the American League crown against the AL East champions, the Baltimore Orioles proved too much for the Twins. Minnesota was swept three straight by an Oriole team that won an incredible 109 regular-season games that year.

The Twins repeated in 1970 as AL West champs behind powerful hitting and solid pitching. Jim Perry won the Cy Young Award as the best pitcher in baseball. Unfortunately, the Twins ran into Baltimore

Rod Carew was the top vote-getter in balloting for the starting lineup of the 1975 American League All-Star Team.

again in the American League Championship Series (ALCS). The Twins were swept in three games.

An era of great baseball in Minnesota had ended. Some Twins stars began to retire, others were traded, and some left the team for more money via free agency. Soon, the Twins found themselves in the AL West cellar, and fans stopped coming to the games.

In 1982, the team moved indoors to the Metrodome. Although the dome attracted fans, it didn't guarantee wins. The team lost a franchise-record 102 games.

In 1984, Twins owner Calvin Griffith sold the team that had been his family's business since 1901. Minneapolis banker Carl Pohlad became the new owner, guaranteeing the Twins would stay in Minnesota.

With the sale of the team came some promising young talent, and the Twins became competitive. Hard-hitting outfielder Kirby Puckett led the way. Pitcher Frank Viola, first baseman Kent Hrbek, third baseman Gary Gaetti, outfielder Tom Brunansky, and shortstop Greg Gagne also helped produce a winner.

Twins' All-Star outfielder Kirby Puckett.

The Stub

Kirby Puckett was among baseball's most popular—and talented—players. The All-Star outfielder won an AL batting title, a Gold Glove Award, and the All-Star Game's MVP. But most of all, it was Puckett's boyish enthusiasm for the game that fans loved.

Puckett had Major League Baseball's most recognizable shape. He stood 5 feet 8 inches, and weighed 220 pounds. He had a barrel chest and an 18-inch neck. His teammates called him "the Stub."

Kirby grew up on Chicago's tough South Side, where gangs and drugs were everywhere. Puckett could have chosen that route like many around him did. Instead, Puckett worked on baseball and his grades. His hard work paid off. He got a scholarship to play baseball in college.

After impressing the major league scouts, the Twins took a chance and drafted Puckett in 1982. He worked hard in the minors and in 1984 became the Twins' full-time center fielder.

Always wanting to improve his game, Puckett asked Twins' hitting coach, former baseball great Tony Oliva, to help him with his swing. The two worked together, and Kirby became one of the best hitters in the game.

Surrounded by a talented cast, Kirby led the Twins up the ladder to the top of the American League. Within five years, Kirby and the Twins would win two World Series titles.

The 1987 World Series

Rookie manager Tom Kelly had plenty of talent to work with in 1987, thanks to the moves made by General Manager Andy MacPhail—and Carl Pohlad's money.

The team consisted of outfielders Puckett, Dan Gladden, and Brunansky; infielders Hrbek, Steve Lombardozzi, Gagne, and Gaetti; catcher Tim Laudner; and pitchers Viola, Bert Blyleven, Juan Berenguer, and ace reliever Jeff Reardon.

Stocked with well-rounded talent, the team grabbed the AL West crown late in the season, thanks to a 56-25 home-field record. The winning tradition at home would continue into the playoffs.

In the ALCS, the Twins were not given much of a chance against the heavily favored Detroit Tigers. But Minnesota stunned the Tigers in just five games. The Twins won three at home and picked up a crucial game-four road win, featuring solo homers by Puckett and Gagne. Now Minnesota was in its first World Series since 1965.

First baseman Kent Hrbek hits a grand slam home run in Game 6 of the 1987 World Series to help the Twins defeat the St. Louis Cardinals 11-5.

23

The Twins were underdogs against the St. Louis Cardinals in this first World Series to be played indoors. But Minnesota had one big advantage—the "Homerdome," as the Metrodome was now called. If they could stretch the Series to a seventh game, Minnesota would have home-field advantage.

The Twins opened the Series with a bang, beating up the Cardinals 10-1 at the Metrodome, thanks to Gladden's grand slam and a Lombardozzi two-run homer. In Game 2, Gaetti and Laudner cracked homers for the Twins, who bagged an 8-4 victory.

The big news was the noise in the Metrodome. With the Twins' great play came the thunderous cheers of Minnesota fans. The noise was deafening. But now that the Series shifted to the Cardinals' outdoor stadium, could Minnesota win on the road?

The Twins quickly got their answer—and it wasn't one they liked. The Cardinals stormed back, winning three in row and taking a 3-2 Series lead. If St. Louis won one of two games in Minnesota, they would be World Champs.

But that was easier said than done. The Twins returned to the Homerdome and continued their winning ways. In Game 6, Twins' designated hitter Don Baylor hit a two-run homer in the fifth. Kent Hrbek sealed the win with a grand-slam in the sixth.

The seventh and deciding game featured some excellent pitching by the Twins. Series MVP Frank "Sweet Music" Viola held the Cardinals to just two runs. Closer Jeff Reardon picked up the save as the Twins won 4-2.

It was the first time the team known as the Twins were World Champions. Minnesota fans had seen great Twins teams come up short, and bad Twins teams sit in the cellar. Finally, Minnesota put everything together and won it all.

Twins players and fans got to savor this title. But they didn't have to wait as long for another one. In 1991, just four seasons later, they were on top again!

Worst To First

After the 1987 World Series Championship, the team faltered quickly. In 1988, the Twins' only bright spot was their attendance. Minnesota became the first franchise in American League history to draw three million fans. In 1989, they slipped below .500. By 1990, the Twins had the worst record in the AL West.

In 1991, the team turned things around. Building around the core group of Puckett, Hrbek, and Gagne, Minnesota acquired more talent.

The Twins celebrate after defeating the Atlanta Braves 1-0 in 10 innings during Game 7 of the 1991 World Series.

Second baseman Chuck Knoblauch came from the minors. He finished the season as Rookie of the Year. Sluggers Mike Pagliarulo and Chilli Davis were acquired from trades. Free-agent pitcher Jack Morris added much-needed leadership to the Twins.

Minnesota put every part of their game together in 1991. They had the best winning percentage in the league (.586), the best team batting average (.280), and the most team hits (1,557). Even more, their pitching was outstanding. Scott Erickson (20-8), Morris (18-12), Kevin Tapani (16-9), and ace closer Rick Aguilera (42 saves) led the way.

After a club-record 16-game winning streak, the Twins ran away with the AL West title. They finished the season eight games ahead of the Chicago White Sox. The Twins were now headed to the ALCS against the AL East Champion Toronto Blue Jays.

Just like the 1987 ALCS, the Twins dismantled their opponents in five quick games, using their Homerdome to full advantage. It was now on to the World Series, where they would face another team that had gone from worst to first: the Atlanta Braves.

In one of the greatest and most exciting World Series in baseball history, the Twins won a nailbiter in seven games. The home team won every game. Fortunately for the Twins, they played four out of the seven at the Homerdome, where the fans were louder than ever.

Five of the seven games were decided by a single run. The last two went to extra innings. In Game 6, Puckett hit an 11th-inning homer to force a seventh game. And in a thrilling final game, Morris pitched a 10-inning, 1-0 shutout. Morris received the Series MVP.

The Twins, who had gone from worst to first, were the World Champions for the second time in five years!

A joyful Kirby Puckett, key member of the 1991 World Champion Minnesota Twins.

Kirby Says Good-bye

In 1992, the World Champs won 90 games and were in a pennant race with the Oakland A's. The A's pulled away in mid-September, but the Twins still led the majors in hitting with a .277 average.

The next few seasons the Twins began to fall. By 1995, Minnesota finished 44 games out of first place, tied for the worst record in all of baseball. One bright spot from that season was the solid hitting, speed, and defensive skill of Marty Cordova, who was named Rookie of the Year.

The Twins were determined to make a run for the pennant in 1996. They acquired All-Star Paul Molitor to go along with Kirby Puckett for solid veteran leadership. The young talent of Chuck Knoblauch, Pat Mears, Rich Becker, and Marty Cordova were to supply the offense needed to win games.

The Twins looked like a real threat in spring training. Puckett and Molitor were happy to be playing together and the young players were playing like veterans. But then Puckett woke one morning and couldn't see out of his right eye. After four months of waiting, Kirby never regained full sight. Kirby Puckett announced his retirement on July 12, 1996.

Many Minnesota Twins fans watched Puckett's retirement press conference with wet eyes. Minnesota's greatest athlete would never wear a Twins uniform again. He was loved not only because he brought the team two championships, but because he was a great guy who loved to play the game. He knew how to make people laugh in the clubhouse, and how to put a smile on a sick child's face in the hospital.

In an age of agents and free agents, of big money and impatience, with players skipping from city to city in search of brighter lights and a few million extra bucks, Puckett sacrificed the glamour and money to stay with his team. "Some are proud to wear the Yankee pinstripes, others bleed Dodger blue," he said. "I'm proud to have worn only one jersey—I'm proud to have been a Minnesota Twin.

"I want to say to the little kids who prayed for me that just because I can't see doesn't mean that God doesn't answer prayers. He answers prayers. I'm able to see out of my one eye, so that's a prayer in itself right there."

On a day that should have been sad, Puckett was the upbeat man who put it all in perspective. "I lived out my dream. What more can I ask?"

The Minnesota Twins lost a genuine star who can never be replaced. But the Twins will continue to build. Carl Pohlad is ready to spend money to sign more free-agents. And the Twins' minor league system is stocked with tremendous talent. It shouldn't be long before the Twins are back on top.

Glossary

All-Star: A player who is voted by fans as the best player at one position in a given year.

American League (AL): An association of baseball teams formed in 1900 which make up one-half of the major leagues.

American League Championship Series (ALCS): A best-of-seven-game playoff with the winner going to the World Series to face the National League Champions.

Batting Average: A baseball statistic calculated by dividing a batter's hits by the number of times at bat.

Earned Run Average (ERA): A baseball statistic which calculates the average number of runs a pitcher gives up per nine innings of work.

Fielding Average: A baseball statistic which calculates a fielder's success rate based on the number of chances the player has to record an out.

Hall of Fame: A memorial for the greatest baseball players of all time located in Cooperstown, New York.

Home Run (HR): A play in baseball where a batter hits the ball over the outfield fence scoring everyone on base as well as the batter.

Major Leagues: The highest ranking associations of professional baseball teams in the world, currently consisting of the American and National Baseball Leagues.

Minor Leagues: A system of professional baseball leagues at levels below Major League Baseball.

National League (NL): An association of baseball teams formed in 1876 which make up one-half of the major leagues.

National League Championship Series (NLCS): A best-of-seven-game playoff with the winner going to the World Series to face the American League Champions.

Pennant: A flag which symbolizes the championship of a professional baseball league.

Pitcher: The player on a baseball team who throws the ball for the batter to hit. The pitcher stands on a mound and pitches the ball toward the strike zone area above the plate.

Plate: The place on a baseball field where a player stands to bat. It is used to determine the width of the strike zone. Forming the point of the diamond-shaped field, it is the final goal a base runner must reach to score a run.

RBI: A baseball statistic standing for *runs batted in.* Players receive an RBI for each run that scores on their hits.

Rookie: A first-year player, especially in a professional sport.

Slugging Percentage: A statistic which points out a player's ability to hit for extra bases by taking the number of total bases hit and dividing it by the number of at bats.

Stolen Base: A play in baseball when a base runner advances to the next base while the pitcher is delivering his pitch.

Strikeout: A play in baseball when a batter is called out for failing to put the ball in play after the pitcher has delivered three strikes.

Triple Crown: A rare accomplishment when a single player finishes a season leading their league in batting average, home runs, and RBIs. A pitcher can win a Triple Crown by leading the league in wins, ERA, and strikeouts.

Walk: A play in baseball when a batter receives four pitches out of the strike zone and is allowed to go to first base.

World Series: The championship of Major League Baseball played since 1903 between the pennant winners from the American and National Leagues.

Index

31